# FOOTE WAS FIRST!

How One
Curious Woman
Connected
Carbon Dioxide
and Climate Change

Written by **JEN BRYANT**     Illustrated by **AMY JUNE BATES**

Quill Tree Books
*An Imprint of HarperCollinsPublishers*

On a mild May day in 1861, Professor John Tyndall spoke before a group of top scientists in England. Two years earlier, he had experimented with different gases and made a discovery: water vapor and carbon dioxide, both found in ordinary air, trapped the sun's heat and made the earth warmer.

"Nothing, so far as I am aware, has been published on [this]," he claimed.

*Remarkable! Astonishing! Fascinating!* the scientists declared. *Professor Tyndall is the first person to prove it!*

But . . . was he really the first? No, he was not!

Three years before Tyndall's experiments, Eunice Newton Foote, an American, had already proven how gases in our atmosphere trap the sun's heat, a natural process known today as the greenhouse effect.

So why didn't Tyndall give Eunice credit? Why did he claim to be the first?

Like most men in those days, the professor believed women were not curious and could not learn science. (Even some women believed it!)

But from a very young age, Eunice was curious.
*Why do some chickens lay more eggs than others? What makes milk turn to butter? Where does well water come from?*

Growing up on her family's farm, questions sprouted in her mind as quickly as wheat in the fields.

Her brothers and sisters were patient with her.

But as Eunice grew, there were questions they couldn't answer: *Why can I see my breath when it's cold? Why does chimney smoke hover above the house? Why does the air feel heavy before a rain storm? How does fog form? Why are there different kinds of clouds?*

Eunice was curious about these and many other things. She longed to learn more about how the world worked.

And so, at age seventeen, Eunice left home to attend a girls' school in Troy, New York. At that time, there were very few places where girls could learn science.

But Eunice took classes in botany, chemistry, and geology, and learned all about plants, the earth's elements, and rocks. She did experiments in a real laboratory, using the same methods and tools that scientists used.

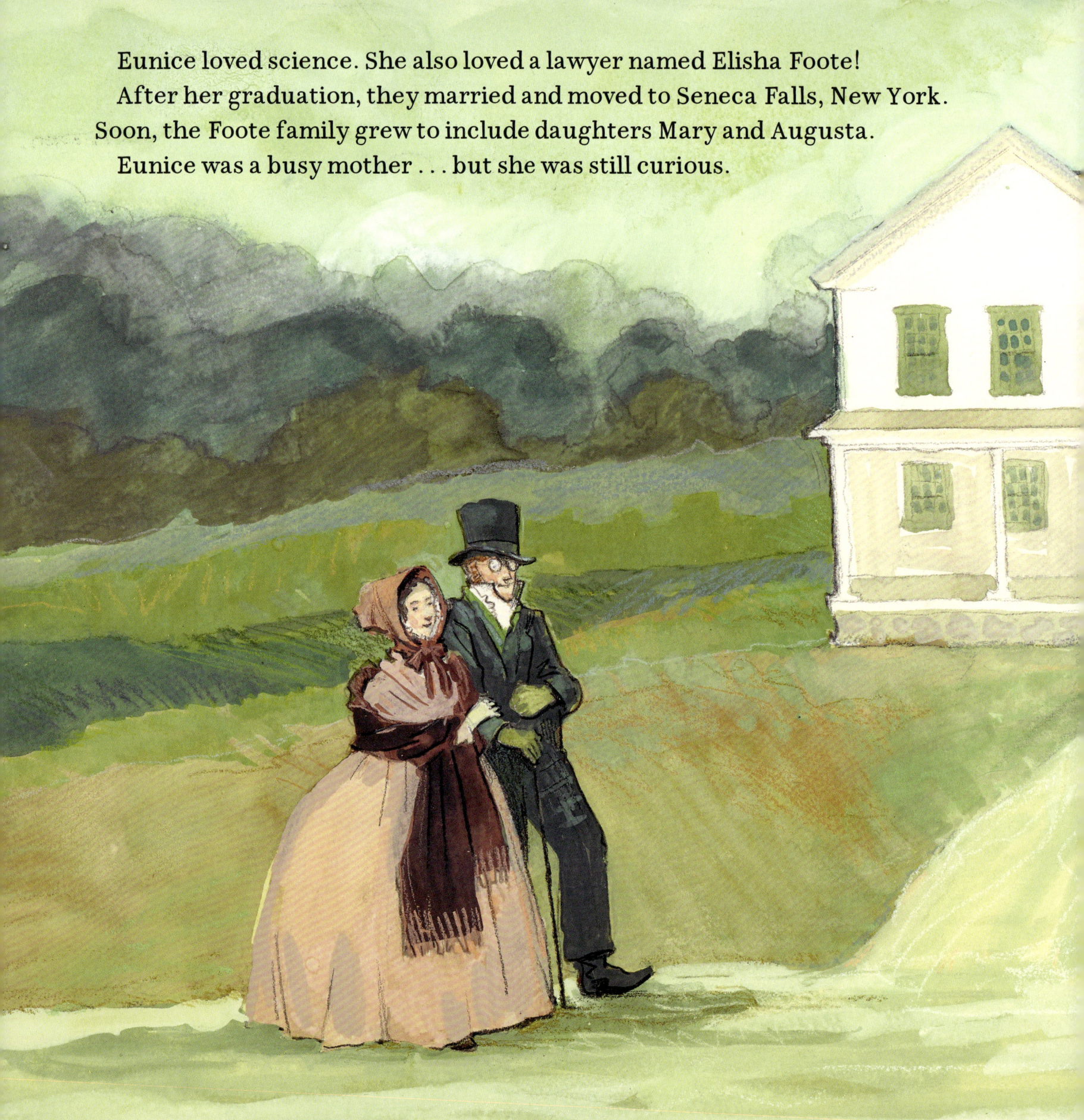

Eunice loved science. She also loved a lawyer named Elisha Foote!
After her graduation, they married and moved to Seneca Falls, New York.
Soon, the Foote family grew to include daughters Mary and Augusta.
Eunice was a busy mother . . . but she was still curious.

On July 17, 1848, Eunice celebrated her twenty-ninth birthday by traveling to the first ever women's rights convention in the United States. People came from near and far to talk about the unequal treatment of women in workplaces, schools, churches, courtrooms, and government.

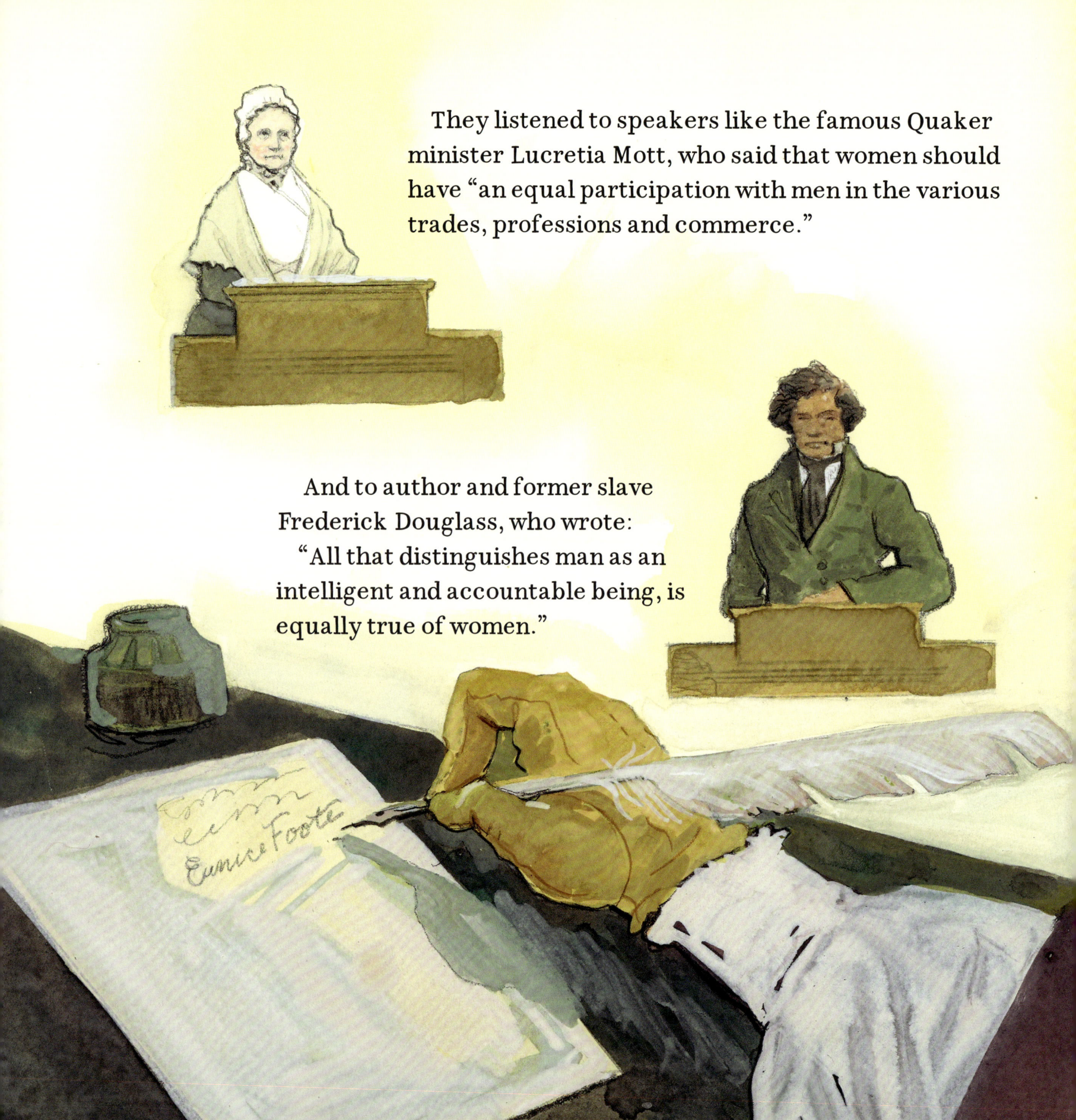

They listened to speakers like the famous Quaker minister Lucretia Mott, who said that women should have "an equal participation with men in the various trades, professions and commerce."

And to author and former slave Frederick Douglass, who wrote: "All that distinguishes man as an intelligent and accountable being, is equally true of women."

Eunice had always been curious, and being curious led to discovering new things. Eunice knew women are just as good as men at that! **But how could she prove it?**

Around this same time, a new branch of science was growing: paleontology.

Paleontologists found fossils of ancient plants and animals, and when they studied these fossils, they noticed differences in their size and shape over time. They concluded that at one time, Earth was much hotter.

Geologists believed that, millions of years ago, the warmer temperatures came from heat beneath the planet's surface.
**But Eunice was curious.** Could there be another reason?

Eunice planned an experiment.

"My investigations have had for their object to determine the different circumstances that affect the thermal action of the rays of light that proceed from the sun."

What happened, she wondered, when sunlight traveled through air that was damp or dry, dense or thin, or mixed with carbon dioxide?

To find out, she took two glass cylinders and placed a thermometer in each.

Using a simple pump, she pulled air out of one cylinder and pushed air into another.

Making sure they were the same temperature, she placed them side by side in the sun.

Later, she checked their temperatures.

The sun's effect, Eunice concluded, "increases with the density of the air, and is diminished as it becomes rarified." In other words, condensed air (like in a valley) got hotter than thin air (like on a mountaintop).

Then she added moisture to one cylinder and made the air in the other one drier. She placed them again in sunlight. "The action of the sun's rays was found to be greater in moist air than dry air," she noted. "Who has not experienced the burning heat of the sun that precedes a summer's shower?" she added.

But the most exciting part of the experiment came next.

After filling one tube with common air and the second with carbon dioxide, she again left them in the sun.

The one with carbon dioxide rose to **125 degrees!**

When she took them out of the sun, the tube with carbon dioxide was "many times as long in cooling" than the tube with common air.

"An atmosphere of that gas would give to our earth a high temperature," she concluded.

And if at some point in the earth's history there had been more carbon dioxide in the air, then it—and not the heat beneath the planet's surface—would have made the earth warmer.

Eunice wrote a report so she could share her methods and her results with other scientists.
**But how? And where?**

Every summer, American scientists held a meeting where they discussed their experiments and discoveries. But only men were allowed to speak at the meetings! Only men could stand before the group and be recognized for their discoveries.

So a friend of Elisha's presented Eunice's results instead.

The date was August 23, 1856.

Perhaps because Eunice was a woman and an American, and because she was not a professional scientist, Tyndall ignored her work. Perhaps he never even read about her experiment (even though her results were published in scientific journals). We will probably never know!

But . . . we *do* know that because Eunice was curious, she was the very *first* person to show us the connection between carbon dioxide and global warming.

As humans have put more and more carbon dioxide into the air from cars, power plants, and factories, our earth has become hotter.

But now we can choose to use what Eunice proved to help our planet: we can find new ways to make the energy we need for our homes, cars, power plants, schools, farms, and factories.

# GLOSSARY

**carbon dioxide:** A colorless gas in the atmosphere, comprised of one part carbon and two parts oxygen. Plants absorb it from the air during photosynthesis.

**common air:** the combination of gases that form the earth's atmosphere

**density:** The amount of mass (how much matter is in an object or a substance) per unit of volume (how much space an object or a substance takes up). A feather pillow has low density because it is lightweight but takes up a lot of space. A brick is high density because it is heavy but takes up relatively little space.

**fossil:** the remains or impression of an organism from a previous age that has been preserved in the earth's crust

**geology:** the study of the earth's crust, including its origins, structure, and processes

**greenhouse effect:** when gases in the earth's atmosphere trap the sun's heat, causing the planet's surface and lower atmosphere to warm

**matter:** any substance that can be weighed and takes up space

**paleontology:** the study of ancient life-forms based on the fossils of plants and animals

**rarified air:** air that is less dense with molecules spread farther apart, as found at higher elevations

# SELECTED BIBLIOGRAPHY

### ARTICLES BY EUNICE NEWTON FOOTE

Foote, Eunice. "Circumstances Affecting the Heat of the Sun's Rays." *The American Journal of Science and Arts* 22, no. 66 (November 1856): 382-83.

Foote, Eunice. "On a New Source of Electrical Excitation." *The London, Edinburgh and Dublin Philosophical Magazine and Journal of Science* 15, no. 99 (1858): 239-40. doi.org/10.1080/14786445808642471.

Foote, Eunice. "Patent Application: Filling for the Soles of Boots and Shoes." US28265A, May 15, 1860. patents.google.com/patent/US28265A/en.

Foote, Eunice. "Patent Application: Improvement in Paper-Making Machines." US45149A, November 22, 1864. patents.google.com/patent/US45149/en?oq=US45149.

### ADDITIONAL SELECTED ARTICLES, BOOKS, AND MANUSCRIPTS

Brazil, Rachel. "Eunice Foote: The Mother of Climate Change." *Chemistry World*, April 20, 2020. www.chemistryworld.com/culture/eunice-foote-the-mother-of-climate-change/4011315.article.

Douglass, Frederick. "The Rights of Women." *The North Star*, July 28, 1848. www.loc.gov/exhibitions/women-fight-for-the-vote/about-this-exhibition/seneca-falls-and-building-a-movement-1776-1890/seneca-falls-and-the-start-of-annual-conventions/frederick-douglass-speaks-in-support.

Emma Willard School Archives. "Troy Female Seminary Catalogs Collection, 1836-1837." www.emmawillard.org/academics/library.

Fleming, James Roger. *Historical Perspectives on Climate Change*. Oxford University Press, 1998.

"Foote's Improved Paper-Making Machine." *American Artisan and Patent Record* 5, no. 19 (November 13, 1867): 298. babel.hathitrust.org/cgi/pt?id=uc1.c2620086&seq=306&q1=Foote%27s+improved+paper-making+machine.

Hecht, Jeff. "Something's a-Foote with Climate Science History: John Tyndall, Eunice Foote, and the Greenhouse Effect." SPIE, March 20, 2020. www.spie.org/news/photonics-focus/marapr-2020/tyndall-foote-and-the-greenhouse-effect?SSO=1.

Huddleston, Amara. "Happy 200th Birthday to Eunice Foote, Hidden Climate Science Pioneer." NOAA Climate.gov, July 17, 2019. www.climate.gov/news-features/features/happy-200th-birthday-eunice-foote-hidden-climate-science-pioneer.

Jackson, Roland. "Eunice Foote, John Tyndall and a Question of Priority." *Notes and Records: The Royal Society Journal of the History of Science*, February 13, 2019. doi.org/10.1098/rsnr.2018.0066.

Leonard, Ermina Newton. *Newton Genealogy, Genealogical, Biographical, Historical: Being a Record of the Descendants of Richard Newton of Sudbury and Marlborough, Massachusetts 1638*. Higginson Book Company, 1915.

Ortiz, Joseph D., and Roland Jackson. "Understanding Eunice Foote's 1856 Experiments: Heat Absorption by Atmospheric Gases." *Notes and Records: The Royal Society Journal of the History of Science*, August 16, 2020. www.royalsocietypublishing.org/doi/abs/10.1098/rsnr.2020.0031.

"Our Roll of Honor. Listing Women and Men Who Signed the Declaration of Sentiments at First Woman's Rights Convention, July 19-20, 1848." Seneca Falls, New York, May 1908. www.loc.gov/item/rbcmiller001182.

Perlin, John. "A 'Foote-Note' on the Hidden History of Climate Science: Why You Have Never Heard of Eunice Foote." Resilience.org, July 30, 2019. www.resilience.org/stories/2019-07-30/a-foote-note-on-the-hidden-history-of-climate-science-why-you-have-never-heard-of-eunice-foote/.

"Report of the Woman's Rights Convention, Held at Seneca Falls, New York, July 19th and 20th, 1848." Seneca Falls Historical Society. cdm16694.contentdm.oclc.org/digital/collection/p16694coll96/id/62.

Rossiter, Margaret W. *Women Scientists in America: Struggles and Strategies to 1940*. Johns Hopkins University Press, 1982.

Sorenson, Raymond P. "Eunice Foote's Pioneering Research on CO2 and Climate Warming." Search and Discovery, January 31, 2011. www.searchanddiscovery.com/documents/2011/70092sorenson/ndx_sorenson.pdf.

"Scientific Ladies–Experiments with Condensed Gases." *Scientific American* 12, no. 1 (September 13, 1856): 5. www.hillheat.com/2023/02/01/scientific-ladies–-experiments-with-condensed-gases.

Schwartz, John. "Overlooked No More: Eunice Foote, Climate Scientist Lost to History." *New York Times*, April 21, 2020. www.nytimes.com/2020/04/21/obituaries/eunice-foote-overlooked.html.

Tyndall, John. "The Bakerian Lecture: On the Absorption and Radiation of Heat by Gases and Vapours, and on the Physical Connexion of Radiation, Absorption, and Conductivity." *Philosophical Transactions of the Royal Society* 151 (1861): 1-36. web.gps.caltech.edu/~vijay/Papers/Spectroscopy/tyndall-1861.pdf.

Tyndall, John. "Note on the Transmission of Radiant Heat through Gaseous Bodies." *Proceedings of the Royal Society of London* 10 (1859-1860): 37-39. www.jstor.org/stable/111604.

Wellman, Judith. *The Road to Seneca Falls: Elizabeth Cady Stanton and the First Woman's Rights Convention*. University of Illinois Press, 2004.

Wells, David A., ed. *Annual of Scientific Discovery: or, Year-Book of Facts in Science and Art for 1857*. Lincoln and Gould, 1857.

Wilkinson, Katharine. "The Woman Who Discovered the Cause of Global Warming Was Long Overlooked. . . ." *Time*, July 17, 2019. www.time.com/5626806/eunice-foote-women-climate-science.

### FILM AND VIDEO

Garro, Eric, dir. *Eunice*. YouTube.com, 2018. Video, 11:57.

Perlin, John. *Symposium: Science Knows No Gender? Eunice Foote*. UC Santa Barbara, 2018. Video, 38:19.

### OTHER RELATED BOOKS

American Association for the Advancement of Science. *Tenth Meeting of the Association: Commencing Wednesday Aug. 20, 1856 at 10 O'clock a.m. at Capitol in the City of Albany, Etc.* C. Van Benthuysen, 1856.

Lovering, Joseph, ed. *Proceedings of the American Association for the Advancement of Science, Eleventh Meeting, Held at Montreal, Canada East, August, 1857*. Lovering, 1858.

# NOTES

"Nothing, so far . . . published on [this]": Tyndall, "Note on the Transmission of Radiant Heat through Gaseous Bodies," 37.

"an equal participation . . . commerce": "Report of the Woman's Rights Convention," 12.

"All that distinguishes . . . of women": Douglass, "The Rights of Women."

"My investigations . . . from the sun": Foote, "Circumstances Affecting the Heat of the Sun's Rays," 382.

"increases with . . . becomes rarified": Foote, "Circumstances Affecting the Heat of the Sun's Rays," 382.

"The action . . . summer's shower?": Foote, "Circumstances Affecting the Heat of the Sun's Rays," 382-83.

"many times as long in cooling": Foote, "Circumstances Affecting the Heat of the Sun's Rays," 383.

"An atmosphere . . . high temperature": Foote, "Circumstances Affecting the Heat of the Sun's Rays," 383.

*"An atmosphere of that gas would give to our earth a high temperature."*

—Eunice Newton Foote, 1856

For Alyssa, Amy, Alex, and Allison–with immense gratitude
–J.B.

For Emily
–A.J.B.

## ACKNOWLEDGMENTS

The author wishes to thank the following people for sharing their time and expertise:

Deborah Shapiro, archives technician (reference), Smithsonian Institution Archives, Washington, DC; Nancy Iannucci, archivist, Emma Willard School, Troy, New York; Liz Foote, marine educator and executive director, Project S.E.A.-Link; Barbara Hunt and Judi Stewart, genealogy volunteers, East Bloomfield Historical Society; John Perlin, author and visiting scholar, UC Santa Barbara; Sarah Principato, PhD, and Rud Platt, PhD, Environmental Studies Department, Gettysburg College, Gettysburg, Pennsylvania; Alexandra Cooper, editor; Shona McCarthy and Mikayla Lawrence, production editors; Joan Giurdanella, copy editor; Marisa Rother, designer; Jeanne Hogle, art director; Amy June Bates, illustrator extraordinaire. And, finally, my wise and patient literary agent, Alyssa E. Henkin, and her husband, Evan Henkin, for his timely suggestion of this topic.

The illustrator would like to thank Dr. Cindy Samet, professor emeritus of chemistry at Dickinson College, for her thoughtful advice, and the Dickinson College Archives & Special Collections for allowing access to their Victorian chemistry equipment collection.

HarperCollins Children's Books, a division of HarperCollins Publishers, 195 Broadway, New York, NY 10007

HarperCollins Publishers, Macken House, 39/40 Mayor Street Upper, Dublin 1, D01 C9W8, Ireland

Quill Tree Books is an imprint of HarperCollins Publishers.

Foote Was First!: How One Curious Woman Connected Carbon Dioxide and Climate Change
Text copyright © 2026 by Jen Bryant
Illustrations copyright © 2026 by Amy June Bates
All rights reserved. Manufactured in Capriate San Gervasio, Italy.
No part of this book may be used or reproduced in any manner whatsoever without written permission except in the case of brief quotations embodied in critical articles and reviews. Unauthorized use of this publication to train generative AI is prohibited and this publication is excluded from the EU's text and data mining exception.
harpercollins.com

Library of Congress Control Number: 2025944963
ISBN 978-0-06-295706-1

The artist used watercolors and colored pencils to create the illustrations for this book.
Typography by Marisa Rother
25 26 27 28 29 RTLO 10 9 8 7 6 5 4 3 2 1

First Edition

# TIMELINE

**1770**
Horace Bénédict de Saussure, a Swiss scientist, describes the warming effect of air inside a glass tube.

**July 17, 1819**
The eleventh of twelve children, Eunice Newton is born to Theresa and Isaac Newton Jr. in Goshen, Connecticut.

**1836–1838**
Eunice attends Troy Female Seminary in Troy, New York, and the nearby Rensselaer School, where she learns how to conduct laboratory experiments.

**August 12, 1841**
Eunice marries Elisha Foote in East Bloomfield and later moves to Seneca Falls, New York.

**July 21, 1842**
Their daughter Mary is born.

**October 24, 1844**
Their daughter Augusta is born.

**July 19–20, 1848**
Eunice attends the first women's rights convention, held in Seneca Falls, and is the fifth signer of its "Declaration of Sentiments and Resolutions" and coeditor of its published proceedings.

**1850s**
Eunice conducts a series of experiments (exact dates unknown) to determine the heating effect of the sun's rays on various gases.

**August 23, 1856**
Professor Joseph Henry of the Smithsonian Institution presents Eunice Foote's paper "Circumstances Affecting the Heat of the Sun's Rays" at the tenth annual American Association for the Advancement of Science (AAAS) conference in Albany, New York.

**September 13, 1856**
Eunice's experiments and results are included in an article published in *Scientific American*, entitled "Scientific Ladies–Experiments with Condensed Gases."

**November 1857**
David A. Wells publishes a summary of Eunice's 1856 gas experiment and results in his *Annual of Scientific Discovery*.

**May 1859**
Irish physicist John Tyndall reports the results of his experiments with radiant energy and its absorption by various gases to the Royal Society of London. He claims to be the first person to conduct such experiments.

**February 7, 1861**
John Tyndall, in his Bakerian Lecture for the Royal Society of London, provides quantitative analysis from his experiments linking the concentration of carbon dioxide in the atmosphere to climate.

**October 22, 1883**
Elisha dies in St. Louis, Missouri, and is later buried in Green-Wood Cemetery, Brooklyn, New York.

**September 30, 1888**
Eunice dies in Lenox, Massachusetts, aged sixty-nine, and is later buried with Elisha.

**January 2011**
Raymond P. Sorenson, a retired petroleum geologist, publishes a paper in *AAPG Search and Discovery*, highlighting Eunice's early (and first) contribution to the understanding of climate change and the presence of carbon dioxide.

**May 17, 2018**
Professor John Perlin gives the presentation "Science Knows No Gender? In Search of Eunice Foote . . ." at a symposium at the University of California, Santa Barbara.

**July 2019**
During the 200th anniversary year of the birth of Eunice Newton Foote, the *New York Times*, *Smithsonian Magazine*, and *Time* magazine pay tribute to her work. Sotheby's sells at auction the first printing of her essay "Circumstances Affecting the Heat of the Sun's Rays" in the November 1856 issue of *The American Journal of Science and Arts* for $4,750.

**April 21, 2020**
The *New York Times* publishes a lengthy article on Eunice Foote in their "Overlooked" series.